Tiny Talks

Volume 8
I Am a Child of God

A year's worth of simple messages that can be given during Primary or Family Home Evening

Other children's books by Lee Ann Setzer

I Am Ready for Baptism

A fun activity book for children preparing for baptism.

Sariah McDuff: Primary Program Diva

The annual Primary program in sacrament meeting seems like the perfect place for Sariah to try out her new superstar rock singer act!

Sariah McDuff: Christmas Detective

What do you get for the girl who doesn't want anything that most kids want? Sariah, her offbeat family, and her funny Primary class find the true spirit of Christmas.

Sariah McDuff: Valentine's Day Scrooge

What is the true meaning of Valentine's Day if you're seven years old and you hate boys?

Sariah McDuff Will Walk with You

The Primary president wants Sariah to make friends with a girl who's very different.

Tiny Talks

Volume 8
I Am a Child of God

**A year's worth of simple messages
that can be given during Primary
or Family Home Evening**

by Lee Ann Setzer
Illustrated by Glenn Harmon

CFI
Springville, Utah

ISBN: 978-1-59955-076-3

Published by CFI,
an imprint of Cedar Fort, Inc.
2373 W. 700 S, Springville, Utah, 84663
www.cedarfort.com

Distributed by:

Cover design © 2007 by Lyle Mortimer
Illustrations © 2007 by Glenn Harmon

Printed in the United States of America
10 9 8 7 6 5 4 3 2 1

Printed on acid-free paper

For my family

All of you are children of the most High.
—Psalm 82:6

Table of Contents

Introduction

Welcome to Tiny Talks 2008!

This year's Primary theme is "I Am a Child of God." Because our Father in Heaven loves us, He wants us to know "all that [we] should do to live with Him someday." That means learning the gospel of Jesus Christ!

This book of talks is very helpful in case of emergency—when someone forgets until Sunday morning that he or she was supposed to give a talk in Primary! But it's also meant as a useful resource for reading, thinking, and talking about the gospel. Each weekly theme includes a talk, a thought question, a visual aid from the Gospel Art Picture Kit, and a scripture.

I hope you enjoy this little book!

—Lee Ann Setzer

Chapter 1

January: I am a child of God. He has a plan for me.

All human beings—male and female—are created in the image of God. Each is a beloved spirit son or daughter of heavenly parents, and, as such, each has a divine nature and destiny.

—"Proclamation," paragraph 2

1. I am a child of God. I lived with Him in the premortal word. I am created in His image.

Scripture

Now the Lord had shown unto me, Abraham, the intelligences that were organized before the world was; and among all these there were many of the noble and great ones . . . and he said unto me: Abraham, thou art one of them; thou wast chosen before thou wast born (Abraham 3:22–23).

The prophet Abraham saw a vision of our premortal life with Heavenly Father. He saw Heavenly Father choose some righteous spirits. They would be leaders and teachers on earth. Abraham learned that he was chosen to be a prophet before he was born (see Abraham 3:22–23).

We lived with our Heavenly Parents and Jesus before we were born. Like Abraham, each person received a special job and special gifts from Heavenly Father. If you are especially good at singing or dancing, loving or serving, running or jumping, smiling or helping, that is a gift from Heavenly Father. He sent us to Earth to grow and serve.[1]

Thought Question: What is one special talent or gift Heavenly Father has given you?

Visual Aid:

GAPK 600
The World

2. I learned of and accepted Heavenly Father's plan. I have a divine destiny.

In the Council in Heaven, our Father explained His plan of salvation. He would help us to become like Him. We were happy and excited to learn our divine destiny.

As a boy, Elder Dieter F. Uchtdorf had to learn English in school. He didn't like English. No one thought he was any good at it. But he loved airplanes. He wanted to grow up to be a pilot. One day, he found out that to become a pilot, he needed to learn English. He said, "Overnight, to the surprise of everybody, it appeared as if my mouth had changed. I was able to learn English."[2]

When Elder Uchtdorf knew what he wanted to become, he did everything he could to reach that destiny. When we know our eternal destiny, we will do everything we can to return to live with our Father in Heaven.

Thought Question: How does knowing your destiny help you make good choices?

Scripture

We will go down, for there is space there, and we will take of these materials, and we will make an earth whereon these may dwell. And we will prove them herewith, to see if they will do all things whatsoever the Lord their God shall command them (Abraham 3:24–25).

Visual Aid:
GAPK 600
The World

3. Heavenly Father gave me agency. I chose to follow His plan.

Scripture

Therefore, cheer up your hearts, and remember that ye are free to act for yourselves—to choose the way of everlasting death or the way of eternal life (2 Nephi 10:23).

In the premortal council, Heavenly Father gave us our agency. Agency is the right to make our own choices.

Think about the words *force* and *choose*. Do you like it when someone forces you to do something? How about when you get to choose what you will do?[3]

Look at this picture. Jesus said, "Behold, I stand at the door, and knock: if any man hear my voice, and open the door, I will come in to him" (Revelation 3:20). The door in the picture does not have a doorknob on the outside. Jesus will not force His way into our lives. He lets us choose to open the door and let Him in. When we invite Him into our lives, He can help us, bless us, and lead us home to Heavenly Father.

Thought Question: What choices have you made today?

Visual Aid:

GAPK 237
Jesus at the Door

4

4. As part of the plan, Jesus created this world for all of God's children. Adam and Eve were our first parents.

Heavenly Father and Jesus created the whole world. They made light and darkness, water and land, plants and animals. Last of all, Heavenly Father created Adam and Eve. He put them in the Garden of Eden. He told them that the earth was for them. He also told them to take good care of it. (See Moses 2:26–30, 3:15.)

Think about all the wonderful things Heavenly Father has made. He created everything we eat and drink. He even made the air we breathe. He expects us to take good care of the earth, just as He expected Adam and Eve to do. We can show our gratitude by enjoying all His beautiful creations. We can also be careful to use these blessings well.

Thought Question: How can you take good care of the earth?

Scripture
And I, the Lord God, took the man, and put him into the Garden of Eden, to dress it, and to keep it (Moses 3:15).

Visual Aid:
GAPK 100 Creation
Living Creatures

Chapter 2

February: The scriptures teach me about Heavenly Father and Jesus Christ and how to return to Them.

For my soul delighteth in the scriptures, and my heart pondereth them, and writeth them for the learning and the profit of my children.

—2 Nephi 4:15

1. The Bible and the Book of Mormon testify of Jesus Christ.

Scripture

Wherefore murmur ye, because that ye shall receive more of my word? Know ye not that the testimony of two nations is a witness unto you that I am God, that I remember one nation like unto another? Wherefore, I speak the same words unto one nation like unto another. And when the two nations shall run together the testimony of the two nations shall run together also (2 Nephi 29:8).

Visual Aid:

GAPK 326
The Bible and Book of Mormon:
Two Witnesses

We have four main books of scripture in the Church. They are the Old Testament, the New Testament, the Bible, and the Doctrine and Covenants. They were written at different times, in different places, for different people. But all the scriptures have one thing in common. All scripture testifies of Jesus Christ.

For a long time, only one book of scripture taught about the Savior. That was the Bible—the Old and New Testaments. But then Heavenly Father helped Joseph Smith translate the Book of Mormon. Now the world had two wonderful books to testify of Jesus Christ! The Book of Mormon shows that the stories about Jesus in the Bible are true. It also helps us understand the Bible better.

We are blessed to have both the Bible and the Book of Mormon to teach us about the Savior.

Thought Question: Why are two testimonies of Jesus Christ better than one?

8

2. Bible stories teach me how to live the gospel.

The New Testament teaches us about Jesus' mortal life. It only tells us a little about Jesus' childhood. But we can learn a lot from what the scriptures do say.

Jesus learned how to live in a family and how to help at home. Joseph taught him how to be a carpenter. Jesus also learned the scriptures and the gospel.

Luke 2:52 says that "Jesus increased in wisdom and stature, and in favour with God and man." To grow in wisdom means to read and think and talk about important ideas, especially the scriptures. To grow in stature means to grow up strong and healthy by taking good care of our bodies. "Favour with God" comes from keeping the commandments and praying often. "Favour with man" comes from being a kind friend and an honest worker.

When we try hard to grow up the way Jesus did, we can become more like Him.

Thought Question: What can I do to grow up like Jesus?

Scripture
And Jesus increased in wisdom and stature, and in favour with God and man (Luke 2:52).

Visual Aid:
GAPK 206
Childhood of Jesus Christ

3. Book of Mormon stories teach me how to live the gospel.

Scripture

And they were all young men, and they were exceedingly valiant for courage, and also for strength and activity; but behold, this was not all—they were men who were true at all times in whatsoever thing they were entrusted (Alma 53:20).

The Book of Mormon tells about Helaman's stripling warriors. A stripling is a young teenage boy. The stripling warriors wanted to help protect their land, their families, and the church during a great war. The prophet Helaman was their leader. He loved them and called them his sons. He said they were brave and strong and true.

After a terrible battle, Helaman was worried about his young warriors. They had never fought before. Had they been hurt or killed? He searched for them and found that every one of them had survived. They told him that their mothers had told them not to doubt. They trusted God, and God protected them (see Alma 53, 56).

The Army of Helaman teaches us that Heavenly Father will help us when we stand strong, trust Him, and keep the commandments.

Thought Question: What can I do to be more like Helaman's stripling warriors?

Visual Aid:

GAPK 313
Two Thousand Young Warriors

4. The Doctrine and Covenants teaches me how to live the gospel.

The Doctrine and Covenants is special because it is the only book of scripture written in our time, for us. In Noah's time, the Lord told Noah to build an ark. In the Book of Mormon, He told Lehi to escape from Jerusalem. In our time, Heavenly Father gave us the Word of Wisdom, in section 89 of the Doctrine and Covenants.

One day, after Joseph Smith had been teaching the leaders of the Church, his wife, Emma, complained about having to clean up their tobacco. The prophet pondered about whether God's servants should be using tobacco. Then he received the Word of Wisdom from Heavenly Father. It warns us that people in our time will try to pull us down using alcohol, tobacco, and other harmful substances. It also teaches us how to choose healthy foods. Finally, it promises health, wisdom, strength, knowledge, and protection to those who keep it.

The Doctrine and Covenants helps us know what Heavenly Father wants for us, today.

Thought Question: How has the Word of Wisdom blessed your life?

Scripture

And all saints who remember to keep and do these sayings, walking in obedience to the commandments, shall receive health in their navel and marrow to their bones; And shall find wisdom and great treasures of knowledge, even hidden treasures; And shall run and not be weary, and shall walk and not faint. And I, the Lord, give unto them a promise, that the destroying angel shall pass by them, as the children of Israel, and not slay them. Amen (D&C 89:18–20).

Visual Aid:

GAPK 405
Emma Smith

Chapter 3

March: Jesus Christ is my Savior.

Follow me, and do the things which ye have seen me do.

—2 Nephi 31:12

1. Jesus Christ is my Savior and the Savior of all mankind.

Scripture

For God so loved the world, that he gave his only begotten Son, that whosoever believeth in him should not perish, but have everlasting life (John 3:16).

On the last night of His life, the Savior went to the Garden of Gethsemane. There, He suffered for the sins of every person in the world—even people who had already died and even people, like us, who weren't born yet. He knew us all. He loved us all. And he suffered for each of us because He loves us. Only God's son could love so much and suffer so much. No one else could have done it for us.

By suffering for our sins, Jesus prepared a way home for us to Heavenly Father. Elder Merrill J. Bateman testifies, "He knows how to help us if we come to Him in faith."[4]

Thought Question: How can you come to the Savior in faith?

Visual Aid:

GAPK 227
Jesus Praying in Gethsemane

14

2. Jesus Christ loves me. Because of His Atonement, I can repent and live with Heavenly Father again.

Committing sins is like carrying around a backpack full of rocks. The Apostle Paul said, "All have sinned, and come short of the glory of God" (Romans 3:23). That means all people need the Savior to take their sins away. Until we give our sins to Him, we carry them around. They chase away the Spirit. They make us feel guilty and unhappy. We may commit more sins because we're trying to cover up the ones we had already. Or we may commit more because we feel bad and grumpy. We try to feel better, but we can't get rid of the sin by ourselves. We need the Savior.

Jesus has already suffered for our sins, because He loves us. He's ready to take away the heavy weight of our sins. But first, we have to have the faith to let Him help us. We have to have the faith to repent.

Thought question: How has repenting helped you feel happier?

Scripture
And if ye believe on his name ye will repent of all your sins, that thereby ye may have a remission of them through his merits (Helaman 14:13).

Visual Aid:
GAPK 227
Jesus Praying in Gethsemane

3. Jesus Christ showed me how to do the will of Heavenly Father.

Scripture

*And as I have prayed among you even so shall ye pray in my church, among my people who do repent and are baptized in my name. Behold I am the light; I have set an example for you
(3 Nephi 18:16).*

Jesus' whole life is an example for us. The Savior once received a message that His good friend Lazarus had died. By the time Jesus reached Lazarus' home, Lazarus had been dead for three days. His sisters were weeping, and Jesus wept with them. Jesus went to the tomb and told the people to open it up.

Then the Savior prayed, "Father, I thank thee that thou hast heard me. And I knew that thou hearest me always: but because of the people which stand by I said it, that they may believe that thou hast sent me." He called Lazarus, and Lazarus walked out of the tomb (John 11:41–43)!

In this story, Jesus prayed so everyone would know that Heavenly Father wants us to pray. Everything Jesus did was an example for us to follow.

Thought question: What is one way I can follow Jesus' example?

Visual Aid:

GAPK 240
Jesus the Christ

4. Jesus Christ lives today. He will come again.

After Jesus died and was resurrected, He visited His apostles and followers several times. At last, He told them to wait in Jerusalem for the Holy Ghost. Then He rose into heaven, until a cloud hid him from His followers. While Jesus' friends were still staring into the sky, two angels came down. They told the people that Jesus would come again. He would come down out of heaven in the same way He'd just risen up (see Acts 1:9–11).

Jesus said that we can recognize the signs that the Second Coming is near. Some signs are fearsome: wars, earthquakes, and great pollutions in the land (D&C 88:87–90). But many signs are hopeful. The restoration of the gospel is one of the signs (D&C 133:36). There will be temples all over the world. All the people in the world will have the chance to hear the gospel in their own language (D&C 133:37). At last, the Savior will come to the earth again.

We can feel hopeful and joyful when we think of the Savior coming again someday.

Thought question: What can I do to get ready for the Second Coming of the Savior?

Scripture

And when he had spoken these things, while they beheld, he was taken up; and a cloud received him out of their sight. And while they looked stedfastly toward heaven as he went up, behold, two men stood by them in white apparel; Which also said, Ye men of Galilee, why stand ye gazing up into heaven? this same Jesus, which is taken up from you into heaven, shall so come in like manner as ye have seen him go into heaven (Acts 1:9–11).

Visual Aid:

GAPK 236
The Ascension of Jesus

Chapter 4

April: I will follow the prophet.

Surely the Lord God will do nothing, but he revealeth his secret unto his servants the prophets.

—Amos 3:7

Scripture

Wherefore, meaning the church, thou shalt give heed unto all his words and commandments which he shall give unto you as he receiveth them, walking in all holiness before me. For his word ye shall receive, as if from mine own mouth, in all patience and faith (D&C 21:4–5).

President Thomas S. Monson told about listening to a gospel lesson in Tonga. The teacher showed the children an octopus lure called a *maka-feke*. Tongan fishermen made them from big rocks and some seashells. The octopus thinks the maka-feke is food and grabs onto it. The fisherman can flip the octopus into the boat because the octopus won't let go.

President Monson said that Satan has many maka-fekes for us. We grab onto bad habits or riches or pride, and we don't want to let go. These maka-fekes look real and good to us. But the prophet can see them more clearly. He can help us stay away from Satan's traps. His words can also help us let go and escape when we've made a mistake.[5]

Thought question: What is one maka-feke the prophet helps you avoid?

Visual Aid:

GAPK 520
Gordon B. Hinckley

2. The prophet teaches me that I should love and forgive others.

President Gordon B. Hinckley told about a woman who showed great forgiveness. As she was driving her car, a young man threw a big frozen turkey at her windshield. It caused a terrible crash. She survived, but she had to have surgery and years of therapy to get back to normal.

She could have been angry and unhappy. But instead, she forgave the young man. She also did all she could to keep him from going to jail for a long time. At his trial, he walked up to her with tears in his eyes. He begged for her forgiveness, and she gave him a big hug.

President Hinckley said, "Forgiveness . . . accomplishes miracles that can happen in no other way."[6] Jesus suffered for us so that we could be forgiven. He wants us to forgive each other, as well.

Thought question: How does forgiveness help both the person forgiving and the person being forgiven?

Scripture

And now, my brethren, seeing that ye know the light by which ye may judge, which light is the light of Christ, see that ye do not judge wrongfully; for with that same judgment which ye judge ye shall also be judged (Moroni 7:48).

Visual Aid:

GAPK 220
The Prodigal Son

3. The prophet teaches me to read and pray about the Book of Mormon.

Scripture

And again, the elders, priests and teachers of this church shall teach the principles of my gospel, which are in the Bible and the Book of Mormon, in the which is the fulness of the gospel (D&C 42:12).

In August of 2005, President Gordon B. Hinckley gave the whole Church a challenge. He asked everyone to read the Book of Mormon by the end of the year. He promised, "If each of you will observe this simple program . . . there will come into your lives and into your homes an added measure of the Spirit of the Lord, a strengthened resolution to [obey] His commandments, and a stronger testimony of the . . . Son of God."[6]

Why is the Book of Mormon so important? It shows that Joseph Smith was really a prophet. It is another testimony that the Bible is true. It shows that people and nations must keep the commandments if they want to be happy and safe. Most of all, it testifies of Jesus Christ, clearly and powerfully.

Thought question: What is your favorite story in the Book of Mormon?

Visual Aid:

GAPK 416
Translating the Book of Mormon

4. The prophet teaches me what I must do to live with God again.

President Gordon B. Hinckley told the Church about the importance of faith. Joseph Smith's faith made him want to pray to know which church was true. Faith helped him publish the Book of Mormon, receive the priesthood, and organize the Church. Faith helped the pioneers across the plains. When the Martin and Willie handcart companies were stranded and dying in the desert, the faithful Saints already in Utah rushed to save them.

President Hinckley said that we can also see faith in small events. He told about his wife's widowed grandmother. One day, her wedding ring slipped off her finger. It was the only thing she had to remember her husband. On her knees, she prayed to find the ring. When she looked down, there it was on the floor.

"Increased faith is what we most need," said President Hinckley. We can follow the prophet by showing faith.[8]

Thought question: What is one experience that has strengthened your faith?

Scripture

If ye have faith as a grain of mustard seed, ye shall say unto this mountain, Remove hence to yonder place; and it shall remove; and nothing shall be impossible unto you (Matthew 17:20).

Visual Aid:

GAPK 415
Helping the Martin Handcart Company across the Sweetwater River

Chapter 5

May: Heavenly Father planned for me to come to a family. I can strengthen my family now.

The family is central to the Creator's plan for the eternal destiny of His children.

—"Proclamation," paragraph 1

Scripture

*A new commandment I give
unto you, That ye love one
another; as I have loved you,
that ye also love one another
(John 13:34).*

Visual Aid:

GAPK 106
Moses in the bulrushes

1. Families in the scriptures teach me how I can strengthen my family.

The prophet Moses' family helped him in his mission as a prophet. When Moses was a baby in Egypt, the king of the land wanted to kill all the Israelite babies. His mother hid him in a little boat, and his older sister Miriam watched over him. The king's daughter found the boat in the river. Miriam stepped out of her hiding place. She asked if the king's daughter needed a nurse for the baby she'd found. Then she took baby Moses to his own mother (see Exodus 2:1–10).

When the Lord called Moses to be a prophet, Moses didn't think he could do it. He told the Lord he couldn't speak very well. The Lord answered by having Moses' brother Aaron speak for Moses. Moses told Aaron what to say, and Aaron told it to the people (see Exodus 4:10–16).

Moses needed help from his family to do his work from the Lord. I can strengthen my family by being loyal, true, and helpful like Miriam, Aaron, and Moses.

Thought question: What can I do to strengthen my family?

2. Each member of my family has a divine role.

In the first verse of the Book of Mormon, Nephi says that he was born of "goodly parents" (1 Nephi 1:1). Nephi and his family showed how each family member has an important role to play.

The Lord told Lehi, Nephi's father, to take his family to live in the wilderness. It was a very hard life. One day, when he was hunting for food, Nephi broke his bow. He could not shoot animals for food. His whole family was sad and angry. Even Lehi, the prophet, was angry at Heavenly Father.

Nephi knew that anger would not help his family. He made a new bow. Then he asked his father where he should go to hunt animals. Lehi repented and prayed for forgiveness. The Lord told him where Nephi should go (see 1 Nephi 16).

Nephi respected his father's role, even when his father made a mistake. He obeyed his father's directions and the Lord's commandments.

Thought question: What is my role in my family?

Scripture

Children, obey your parents in the Lord: for this is right . . . And, ye fathers, provoke not your children to wrath: but bring them up in the nurture and admonition of the Lord (Ephesians 6:1, 4).

Visual Aid:

GAPK 301
Lehi's Family Leaving Jerusalem

3. Scripture study, family prayer, and family home evening can strengthen my family.

Scripture

And they rehearsed unto me the words of their mothers, saying: We do not doubt our mothers knew it (Alma 56:48).

The prophet Helaman led two thousand young warriors into battle. They had never fought before, but they fought so powerfully that they frightened their enemies. They were so strong and righteous that their enemies couldn't hurt them.

The army of Helaman "did not fear death." Helaman said they loved their families' freedom more than their own lives. They told Helaman that their mothers had taught them not to fear. They said, "We do not doubt our mothers knew it." (See Alma 56:44–56.)

Their strength came from good mothers who taught them the gospel. We can find strength and help in our parents' teaching and testimony. Studying the gospel in our families can protect us and help us.

Thought question: How do my parents' teachings strengthen me?

Visual Aid:

GAPK 313
Two Thousand Young Warriors

4. The priesthood can bless and strengthen my family.

Captain Moroni was an army general and a righteous man in the Book of Mormon. He wanted to save his people from their enemies. But the people were too busy fighting and disobeying the commandments. Moroni feared that they would be destroyed because they would not keep the commandments. He knew he had to help his people obey the Lord.

Moroni had to show the people what was truly important. He ripped his coat in half. Then he wrote all the important things on it: "Our God, our religion, and freedom, and our peace, our wives, and our children." He put it on a pole and went from town to town, calling everyone to come and help him. (See Alma 46:11–36.)

Our fathers don't usually rip up their coats. But their job is to protect us, lead us, and teach us. The priesthood gives them the power and the duty to lead us home to Heavenly Father.

Thought question: How can I follow the priesthood in my home?

Scripture

And no man taketh this honour unto himself, but he that is called of God, as was Aaron (Hebrews 5:4).

Visual Aid:

GAPK 312
Captain Moroni Raises the Title of Liberty

Chapter 6

June: The temple is a blessing for me and my family.

And verily I say unto you, let this house be built unto my name, that I may reveal mine ordinances therein unto my people.

—D&C 124:40

Scripture

And Adam and Eve blessed the name of God, and they made all things known unto their sons and their daughters (Moses 5:12).

Visual Aid:

GAPK 119
Adam and Eve Teaching Their Children

1. I will live now to be worthy to go to the temple and do my part to have an eternal family.

Adam and Eve were the first man and woman on the earth. They were also the first parents and the first family. Adam and Eve wanted their children to be happy and follow God. When Adam learned about the plan of salvation, he taught it to his family. Adam and Eve knew that keeping the commandments would help their children to grow up righteous and joyful (see Moses 5:10–12).

We are also part of Heavenly Father's family. He wants us all to return home to live with Him and with our own families. If we work hard to be worthy to enter the temple, our families can be eternal. We can live together forever.

Thought question: What can I do now to prepare for the temple?

2. My tithing helps to build temples.

When Moses led the people of Israel into the wilderness, the Lord commanded them to make a tabernacle. The tabernacle was like a traveling temple, made of tents. The people were very excited to help. Moses told them that the "wise hearted" people should bring gifts to help build the temple. The Spirit filled many people's hearts. They brought gold and silver, jewels and fine wood, fine cloth, and spice and oil. Finally, Moses had to tell them to stop. They had brought more than enough gifts to build the tabernacle! (See Exodus 35–36.)

We can help build temples, too. Our tithing pays for the land, the workers, the flowers and trees, and the beautiful things in the temples. If we give with wise and willing hearts like the Israelites, we can be filled with a joyful spirit, just like they were.

Thought question: How has your tithing helped to build the Church?

Scripture

And they came, every one whose heart stirred him up, and every one whom his spirit made willing, and they brought the Lord's offering to the work of the tabernacle of the congregation, and for all his service, and for the holy garments (Exodus 35:21).

Visual Aid:

GAPK 108
Moses Calls Aaron to the Ministry

3. I will do family history work so my ancestors can receive temple blessings.

Scripture

Thus came the voice of the Lord unto me, saying: All who have died without a knowledge of this gospel, who would have received it if they had been permitted to tarry, shall be heirs of the celestial kingdom of God (D&C 137:7).

The Prophet Joseph Smith had a vision of the celestial kingdom. It was full of light and joy, and the streets were paved with gold. Joseph saw his brother Alvin there, and he was surprised, because Alvin had died before the gospel was restored. Alvin had not had a chance to be baptized. The Lord's voice told Joseph that Alvin "would have received it with all [his] heart" (D&C 137:8).

Many of our ancestors who died without the gospel have heard it in the spirit world. They want to be baptized. They want to be with their families forever. But they need our help to do it. We can find out their names and do their work in the temple. Even if we don't know what to do or where to start, the Spirit will help us do this important work.

Thought question: What is the first thing I could do to start family history work?

Visual Aid:

GAPK 504
Temple Baptismal Font

4. I will be reverent, dress modestly, and speak kindly to be worthy to enter the temple.

Think about a temple, inside and outside. President Boyd K. Packer said that a temple at night, lighted up, is a symbol of the "power and inspiration of the gospel of Jesus Christ."9 Inside, the temple is clean and quiet, beautiful and happy. The Apostle Paul said that our bodies are temples. To be worthy to enter the temple, we should work to be like the temple: clean, joyful, and reverent. (See 1 Corinthians 6:16.)

It may be a few years before we get to enter a temple. But every day, we can make the choices that lead us there. We shine like a temple in the night by being examples of the gospel of Jesus Christ. We can take care of our bodies and dress carefully and modestly. We can live reverently. This doesn't mean we have to whisper all the time. But we should always remember that the people around us are Heavenly Father's children, and treat them kindly. Then we will be worthy to enter the temple someday.

Thought question: What can you do today to be worthy to enter the temple someday?

Scripture

What? know ye not that your body is the temple of the Holy Ghost which is in you, which ye have of God, and ye are not your own (1 Corinthians 6:16)?

Visual Aid:

GAPK 535
Washington D.C. Temple

Chapter 7

July: Because I know we are all children of God, I will share the gospel with others.

And if it so be that you should . . . bring, save it be one soul unto me, how great shall be your joy.

—D&C 18:15

1. I will prepare to be a missionary by praying and reading the scriptures daily.

Scripture

Therefore, verily I say unto you, lift up your voices unto this people; speak the thoughts that I shall put into your hearts, and you shall not be confounded before men (D&C 100:5).

Everyone who has a job has tools to do the job. Mechanics have wrenches. Computer programmers have computers. Missionaries have prayer and the scriptures.

Missionaries pray when they get up. After a little time to eat breakfast and get dressed, they pray and study the scriptures on their own. Then they study the scriptures as companions. Next, they plan their day. They decide which gospel lessons to teach and which scriptures will help their investigators feel the Spirit. Then they pray before they leave home. All day, they teach the gospel, share scriptures, pray with the people they teach, and look for more people to teach. At home again, they pray as companions and they pray on their own.

Prayer is the tool that helps the missionaries feel the Spirit and know what Heavenly Father wants them to do and say. The scriptures help people understand the gospel and feel the Spirit. We can prepare to be missionaries by praying and reading the scriptures.

Visual Aid:

GAPK 617
Search the Scriptures

Thought question: How have prayer and the scriptures helped you feel the Spirit?

2. I will prepare to be a missionary by being faithful and obedient.

Ammon was a missionary in the Book of Mormon. He preached to the Lamanites. He became a servant for the Lamanite king, Lamoni. Lamoni told Ammon to help take care of the sheep. When thieves came, Ammon wouldn't let them take the sheep. He fought the thieves by himself.

Lamoni's servants ran to tell the king. The king could hardly believe it. He asked, "Where is this man that has such great power?" The servants answered, "He is feeding thy horses." The king grew even more amazed. Ammon was powerful enough to chase away the thieves, but he also was humble enough to obey all the king's orders. Because of Ammon's faith and obedience, the king and many of his people repented and accepted the gospel. (See Alma 18.)

Like Ammon, we can share the gospel through our obedience and faithfulness.

Thought question: What is one way you can show your obedience?

Scripture

Let your light so shine before men, that they may see your good works, and glorify your Father which is in heaven (Matthew 5:16).

Visual Aid:

GAPK 310
Ammon Defends the Flocks of King Lamoni

3. Living the gospel standards helps me be a missionary now.

Scripture

Therefore, O ye that embark in the service of God, see that ye serve him with all your heart, might, mind and strength, that ye may stand blameless before God at the last day (D&C 4:2).

When he was just nineteen years old, Joseph F. Smith met up with a crowd of armed, drunken men. They wanted to kill any Mormons they met. Some of the other Saints hid in the bushes, but not Joseph F. Smith. A drunken man pointed his gun at Joseph and asked, "Are you a 'Mormon'?"

Joseph F. Smith looked the man in the eye and said, "Yes, siree; dyed in the wool; true blue, through and through." The surprised man shook Joseph F. Smith's hand and answered, "Well, you are the . . . pleasantest man I ever met! Shake, young fellow. I am glad to see a man that stands up for his convictions." Then the men all rode away on their horses.[10]

One of "My Gospel Standards" says, "I will be honest with Heavenly Father, others, and myself." We can be true and honest like Joseph F. Smith.

Thought question: What other gospel standards can help you be a missionary? How?

Visual Aid:

GAPK 511
Joseph F. Smith

4. I help to bless others when I share the gospel.

Nephi and Lehi were righteous missionaries in the Book of Mormon. Once, the Lamanites threw them in prison with no food. When the Lamanites came to kill them, the Lord made a circle of fire around the missionaries, keeping them safe. No one could touch them.

The Lamanites were very frightened, but Nephi and Lehi told them not to be afraid. The prison began to shake, and it got very dark. Suddenly, a voice told the Lamanites to repent and let the missionaries live. One man, who remembered the gospel, told everyone that they needed to pray until they had faith in Jesus Christ. When they prayed and opened their eyes, they were all surrounded by the fire from heaven! The voice came again, but this time it said, "Peace, peace be unto you, because of your faith in my Well Beloved."

Because of the missionaries' faith, many people received the blessings of the gospel (see Helaman 5).

Thought question: How can you share the gospel now?

Scripture

For I am not ashamed of the gospel of Christ: for it is the power of God unto salvation to every one that believeth; to the Jew first, and also to the Greek (Romans 1:16).

Visual Aid:

GAPK 612
Missionaries Teach the Gospel of Jesus Christ

Chapter 8

August: I will show my faith in Jesus Christ by being baptized and confirmed.

And their children shall be baptized for the remission of their sins when eight years old, and receive the laying on of the hands.

—D&C 68:27

1. I will show my faith by being baptized and confirmed and keeping my baptismal covenants.

Scripture

Now I say unto you, if this be the desire of your hearts, what have you against being baptized in the name of the Lord, as a witness before him that ye have entered into a covenant with him, that ye will serve him and keep his commandments, that he may pour out his Spirit more abundantly upon you (Mosiah 18:10)?

Visual Aid:

GAPK 601
Baptism

A man named Nicodemus came to the Savior to learn the gospel. Jesus taught him that everyone needs to be born again. Nicodemus didn't understand. He asked, "How can a man be born when he is old?" (John 3:4). Then Jesus told him that everyone needs to be "born of water and of the Spirit" (John 3:5).

Jesus was talking about baptism. When we are "born of water," we show that we accept Jesus' sacrifice for us, and He washes away our sins. When we are "born of the Spirit," we receive the Holy Ghost, to guide and help us always. Jesus told Nicodemus that he had to be baptized and receive the Holy Ghost to see the kingdom of God.

Thought question: What can you do to prepare now for baptism?

2. The Holy Ghost will prompt me to repent and live righteously after I am baptized and confirmed.

In New Testament times, a magician named Simon lived in Samaria. Everyone in town thought he was great and powerful. When missionaries came and taught the gospel, Simon was baptized.

Later, Jesus' apostles came to the town. They had the authority to give the gift of the Holy Ghost. When Simon saw this, he "offered them money, saying, Give me also this power" (Acts 8:18–19). The apostles said no. He could not buy the priesthood of God. He could not buy the gift of the Holy Ghost, no matter how much money he had. Simon repented of his unrighteous wish.

Help from the Holy Ghost is help from God Himself. Simon learned that it is worth more than all the money in the world. But Heavenly Father gives it to us freely. The only price is our faith and obedience.

Thought question: How can you invite the Holy Ghost into your life?

Scripture
And also, the voice of the Son came unto me, saying: He that is baptized in my name, to him will the Father give the Holy Ghost, like unto me; wherefore, follow me, and do the things which ye have seen me do (2 Nephi 31:12).

Visual Aid:
GAPK 602
The Gift of the Holy Ghost

And he took bread, and gave thanks, and brake it, and gave unto them, saying, This is my body which is given for you: this do in remembrance of me (Luke 22:19).

Visual Aid:

GAPK 603
Blessing the Sacrament

3. When I take the sacrament, I renew my baptismal covenants.

The last night of the Savior's life was a feast called the Passover. In the Passover, the Jews celebrated a time when the Lord saved them from destruction. During the Passover feast, Jesus prayed, then broke bread and gave it to the apostles. He told them, "This is my body, which is given for you." He told them they should break bread to remember Him (Luke 22:19).

Then, He took the cup and told them they should drink to remember His blood. This was the first sacrament. We still take the bread and water each week, to remember how Jesus saves us from death and sin. We remember our baptisms. We remember our promise to follow the Savior.

Thought question: What can I do during the sacrament to remember the Savior?

4. Heavenly Father forgives all who truly repent.

Just before the Savior came to Earth, Heavenly Father sent two prophets to prepare the people. In Jerusalem, He sent John the Baptist. To the Nephites and Lamanites, He sent Samuel the Lamanite. Both of these prophets preached that the Savior would soon come. And both commanded the people to repent (see Mark 1:4, Helaman 14:13.)

Faith and repentance are the first two principles of the gospel. Like the people long ago, we have to prepare to receive the Savior. We receive His name when we are baptized. To prepare, we must repent. Repentance means recognizing and feeling sorry for anything we've done wrong. We must fix everything we can and pray for forgiveness from Heavenly Father. Then we are ready to receive the Savior through baptism. Then we are on the road home to Heavenly Father, with Holy Ghost to help us.

Thought question: How can repentance help you to feel the Holy Ghost?

Scripture

And again, believe that ye must repent of your sins and forsake them, and humble yourselves before God; and ask in sincerity of heart that he would forgive you; and now, if you believe all these things see that ye do them (Mosiah 4:10).

Visual Aid:

GAPK 314
Samuel the Lamanite on the Wall

Chapter 9

September: I can pray to Heavenly Father, and He will hear and answer my prayers.

Therefore I say unto you, What things soever ye desire, when ye pray, believe that ye receive them, and ye shall have them.

—Mark 11:24

1. I learn about prayer from the scriptures.

When Joseph Smith was a young boy, the people where he lived grew very excited about religion. Leaders of different churches tried to get everyone to come to their church. Sometimes the leaders of the churches would argue with each other. Joseph Smith was very confused. He wanted to know which church was right.

Joseph read the Bible. In James 1:5, he read, "If any of you lack wisdom, let him ask of God, that giveth to all men liberally, and upbraideth not; and it shall be given him." The Holy Ghost spoke to Joseph in his heart. Joseph knew he needed to obey this scripture (see Joseph Smith—History 1:5–13).

Because young Joseph learned about prayer from the scriptures, he prayed to know which church was true, and Heavenly Father answered his prayer.

Thought question: Have you received an answer from Heavenly Father through prayer?

Visual Aid:

GAPK 402
Joseph Smith Seeks Wisdom in the Bible

2. Heavenly Father wants me to pray to Him often—anytime, anywhere.

Two Book of Mormon missionaries named Alma and Amulek once met some people called the Zoramites. The Zoramites had built a tall tower for praying. Each person stood in the tower once a week and prayed exactly the same prayer. Then everyone went home. They didn't think about God again until the next week. Alma and Amulek couldn't believe their eyes! (See Alma 31.)

The rich Zoramites didn't want to hear the gospel. But some poor Zoramites were sad because the rich ones wouldn't let them pray in the tower. They thought they couldn't pray at all. Alma taught them that they could pray in the wilderness and in the fields, at home and by themselves alone. Amulek taught them to pray for mercy and safety, for their crops and flocks, and for their families. They—and we—could pray about anything, anywhere. (See Alma 33 and 34.)

Thought question: Where are some places you can pray?

Scripture

Counsel with the Lord in all thy doings, and he will direct thee for good; yea, when thou liest down at night lie down unto the Lord, that he may watch over you in your sleep; and when thou risest in the morning let thy heart be full of thanks unto God; and if ye do these things, ye shall be lifted up at the last day (Alma 37:37).

Visual Aid:

GAPK 605
Young Boy Praying

3. Heavenly Father knows me. He will answer my prayers in ways that are best for me.

Scripture

Search diligently, pray always, and be believing, and all things shall work together for your good, if ye walk uprightly and remember the covenant wherewith ye have covenanted one with another (D&C 90:24).

Elder Richard G. Scott said that we don't need to worry about how our prayers sounds. "Just talk to your Father," he said. "He hears every prayer and answers it in His way." In our prayers, we tell Heavenly Father our problem and what we want to do about it. Then, "sometimes he answers yes, sometimes no. Often He withholds an answer."

A "yes" answer can be a feeling of "peace" (D&C 6:23) "in your mind and in your heart" (D&C 8:2). A "no" can be a "stupor of thought" (D&C 8:9). Sometimes, Heavenly Father doesn't give us an answer right away. This can show that He trusts us to make a good decision. We shouldn't sit around waiting for an answer. Instead, we should move forward and do the best we can.

We can always trust Heavenly Father to answer our prayers, because He loves us.[11]

Visual Aid:

GAPK 606
Family Prayer

Thought question: What are some of the ways your prayers have been answered?

4. Answers to my prayers come from Heavenly Father through the Holy Ghost, the scriptures, and others.

The Book of Mormon prophet Alma once tried to teach the people in the city of Ammonihah. They would not listen, and they spit on him and finally threw him out of the city. Alma had "labored" in "mighty prayer" for them (Alma 8:10), but at last all he could do was trudge down the road to the next city. He was very discouraged.

As Alma was walking along, an angel came to him. The angel said that Heavenly Father had heard Alma's prayers. He commanded Alma to go back to Ammonihah. Alma "returned speedily" (Alma 8:18) to the city. This time, Heavenly Father had prepared a man named Amulek to help Alma. Together, they delivered Heavenly Father's message to the people.

In this story, a heavenly messenger and another person helped answer Alma's prayers.

Thought question: What is one way your prayers have been answered?

Scripture

But behold, I say unto you that ye must pray always, and not faint; that ye must not perform any thing unto the Lord save in the first place ye shall pray unto the Father in the name of Christ, that he will consecrate thy performance unto thee, that thy performance may be for the welfare of thy soul (2 Nephi 32:9).

Visual Aid:

GAPK 606
Family Prayer

Chapter 10

October: Because I am His child, I will serve God with all my heart, might, mind, and strength.

Therefore, O ye that embark in the service of God, see that ye serve him with all your heart, might, mind and strength, that ye may stand blameless before God at the last day.

—D&C 4:2

And that thou mayest more fully keep thyself unspotted from the world, thou shalt go to the house of prayer and offer up thy sacraments upon my holy day; For verily this is a day appointed unto you to rest from your labors, and to pay thy devotions unto the Most High (D&C 59:9–10).

Visual Aid:

GAPK 617
Search the Scriptures

1. I will serve God by doing things on the Sabbath that will help me feel close to Heavenly Father and Jesus.

Have you ever seen a windup clock? Instead of a battery, a windup clock has a key on the back. You wind it up, and it runs for a day, or for several days. Then it starts to wind down. It moves more slowly, and after a while it doesn't run at all, unless you wind it up again. Elder Dean L. Larsen said that our spirits need rewinding, just like a windup clock.

Once a week, Heavenly Father gives us a chance to "rewind." We take the sacrament. We learn and serve others in Primary. The rest of the day is also for Heavenly Father, not just for playing or lying around. We can read the scriptures and other good books. We can visit family members or people who can't go out. We can write in our journals and work on our family history.

By using the Sabbath well, we can wind up our spiritual clocks for the rest of the week![12]

Thought question: What will you do this week on the Sabbath to wind up your spiritual clock?

2. I can serve Heavenly Father by serving others.

Jesus said that someday He will judge the world. He will separate out the righteous people. He will tell the righteous people that they fed Him when He was hungry. They gave Him a drink when He was thirsty. They gave Him a home when He was a stranger. They gave Him clothes when He had none. And they visited Him in prison.

The righteous people will be confused. They will not remember helping the Lord. The Lord will answer, "Inasmuch as ye have done it unto one of the least of these my brethren, ye have done it unto me." (See Matthew 25:40.) Whenever we are kind to someone, we are showing our love for Heavenly Father and Jesus.

Thought question: How have you helped someone else this week?

Scripture

And the King shall answer and say unto them, Verily I say unto you, Inasmuch as ye have done it unto one of the least of these my brethren, ye have done it unto me (Matthew 25:40).

Visual Aid:

GAPK 218
The Good Samaritan

3. The prophets and apostles teach me how to serve.

Scripture

For, brethren, ye have been called unto liberty; only use not liberty for an occasion to the flesh, but by love serve one another (Galatians 5:13).

When Elder L. Tom Perry was a boy, his father was a bishop. Many families in the ward needed help. The bishop's job was to deliver flour, sugar, wheat, and other food. Elder Perry had gotten a little red wagon for Christmas. Elder Perry's job was to load up the red wagon. Then, he says, "The two of us, walking and talking together, would complete our welfare assignment."[13]

Parents and their sons and daughters can learn from Elder Perry's talk. Parents should help children learn to serve. Elder Perry was only six years old when he helped his father. Even young children can serve together with their parents.

Thought question: What could you do to serve someone today?

Visual Aid:

GAPK 615
Serving One Another

4. Because others serve me, I too want to serve.

A young man in Chile joined the Church, but he decided not to attend church or keep the commandments anymore. At first, he had plenty of money, and everything seemed fine. But soon he lost his job, and he had to start taking care of his mother and little brother when his father died. He said, "Everything seemed to grow dark around me." Finally, he returned to the Church.

He learned at church about a new program called the Perpetual Education Fund. The program helps people get an education so they can take care of their families. He wanted to apply, but he wondered if they would take someone like him. He was very happy when he was accepted to the program!

He said, "Since then, I have done everything in my power to show my gratitude." He works and studies hard and serves in the Church. He is happy that the Lord has forgiven him, and now he wants to serve others.[14]

Thought question: How has the Lord blessed you? How can you serve others?

Scripture
Bear ye one another's burdens, and so fulfil the law of Christ (Galatians 6:2).

Visual Aid:
GAPK 616
Family Togetherness

Chapter 11

November: I am thankful to know that we are all children of God.

Thou shalt thank the Lord thy God in all things.

—D&C 59:7

1. I am thankful to be a beloved child of God.

Scripture

I have said, Ye are gods; and all of you are children of the most High (Psalm 82:6).

President Thomas S. Monson told a story about a woman who was very discouraged. She had made some terrible mistakes and committed many sins. She thought that no one could forgive her. Her church leader wanted to help. He saw a picture of a young lady on the woman's dresser. He asked who it was. The woman said, "She is my daughter, the one beautiful thing in my life." He asked if the woman would forgive her daughter if she made a mistake. Would she help her? "Of course I would! I would do anything for her!" the woman answered.

President Monson told her, "Figuratively speaking, Heavenly Father has a picture of you on His dresser. He loves you and will help you. Call upon Him."

Heavenly Father knows our names. He knows what we're going through, and He knows how we feel. We can always ask Him for help.[15]

Thought question: What can you do to remember that you are a child of God?

Visual Aid:

GAPK 607
Young Girl speaking at Church

2. I am thankful for my body. I know my body is a temple.

The brother of Jared was a great Book of Mormon prophet. His people were commanded to cross the sea in wooden barges with no windows. When the brother of Jared prayed for light in the barges, the Lord told him to think of an answer to the problem. The brother of Jared made sixteen small glass stones. Then he prayed for the Lord to touch them and make them shine (see Ether 2).

When the Lord touched the stones, the brother of Jared saw first His finger, then His Spirit body. The prophet learned that our bodies look like Heavenly Father's body. The Lord said, "All men were created in the beginning after mine own image" (Ether 3:15).

Our bodies are sacred because they are in the image of God. We need to take good care of them. We should keep them strong, clean, and healthy.

Thought question: What can you do to show respect for your body?

Scripture

And never have I showed myself unto man whom I have created, for never has man believed in me as thou hast. Seest thou that ye are created after mine own image? Yea, even all men were created in the beginning after mine own image (Ether 3:15).

Visual Aid:

GAPK 318
The Brother of Jared Sees the Finger of the Lord

*For none of these iniqui-
ties come of the Lord; for
he doeth that which is good
among the children of men;
and he doeth nothing save it
be plain unto the children of
men; and he inviteth them all
to come unto him and par-
take of his goodness; and he
denieth none that come unto
him, black and white, bond
and free, male and female;
and he remembereth the hea-
then; and all are alike unto
God, both Jew and Gentile
(2 Nephi 26:33).*

Visual Aid:

GAPK 311
The Anti-Nephi-Lehies Burying
Their Swords

3. Heavenly Father loves all of His children.

King Mosiah in the Book of Mormon had four sons. King Mosiah was growing old. The people wanted him to say which son should become the new king. But none of the sons wanted to be king. They had strong testimonies of the gospel. They wanted to teach the gospel to the Lamanites (see Mosiah 28:1).

The Nephites laughed at them. They said the Lamanites wouldn't listen. They thought the wicked Lamanites would never accept the gospel. They even wanted to go kill the Lamanites (see Alma 26:23–25.) But the sons of Mosiah trusted God. They preached to the Lamanites for fourteen years. Thousands of Lamanites accepted the gospel because the sons of Mosiah loved people who were very different from them.

Thought question: Have you had an experience making friends with someone from another culture, reli-gion, or country?

4. I can show respect and kindness to all of God's children.

Jesus taught the people in Jerusalem that Heavenly Father notices when a tiny sparrow dies. Then He said, "Fear not; ye are of more worth than many sparrows" (Matthew 10:29–31). Every one of us matters to Heavenly Father. Jesus showed that he loved and respected all Heavenly Father's children. People in Jerusalem didn't like Samaritans, but Jesus healed a Samaritan. People with a terrible disease called leprosy had to live outside the city, and no one would go near them. But Jesus spoke with and healed them (Luke 17:12–16).

A woman who had committed many sins kissed and cleaned Jesus' feet. People wondered if Jesus knew what the woman had done. Jesus did know—but he loved the woman and forgave her (Luke 7: 36–50). The Romans had conquered Jerusalem, but Jesus healed a Roman soldier's servant (Matthew 8:5–13).

We can follow Jesus' example by being kind to people who are different or left out.

Thought question: How can I show greater love to Heavenly Father's children?

Scripture
And be ye kind one to another, tenderhearted, forgiving one another, even as God for Christ's sake hath forgiven you (Ephesians 4:32).

Visual Aid:
GAPK 218
The Good Samaritan

Chapter 12

December: I love my Savior, Jesus Christ, and His restored gospel.

And we talk of Christ, we rejoice in Christ, we preach of Christ, we prophesy of Christ, and we write according to our prophecies.

—2 Nephi 25:26

1. The prophets foretold Jesus Christ would come to the earth.

Scripture

For, for this intent have we written these things, that they may know that we knew of Christ, and we had a hope of his glory many hundred years before his coming; and not only we ourselves had a hope of his glory, but also all the holy prophets which were before us (Jacob 4:4).

Visual Aid:

GAPK 113
Isaiah Writes of Christ's Birth

Thousands of years before Jesus was born, prophets knew that He would come to the earth. Enoch was one prophet who saw a vision of the Savior. He saw God's children living wickedly, and he saw Heavenly Father weep. Enoch wept, too, because he saw the wicked people punished. Then he saw the Savior come. Enoch felt happy. He thought that there would be peace on the earth.

But then Enoch saw the people kill Jesus. He wept again. When would Heavenly Father let the Earth rest? At last, he saw the Savior come again. He saw peace in the earth, and he felt joy.

Enoch taught his people about the Savior thousands of years before Jesus was born (see Moses 7: 20-67.)

Thought question: Why did Heavenly Father tell the prophets about the Savior so many years before He came to earth?

2. The prophecies were fulfilled. Jesus Christ was born and the righteous rejoiced.

The Bible teaches about two righteous people who waited for the Savior to come. The Lord had promised Simeon that he would see the Savior before he died. When Jesus' parents brought him to the temple, the Spirit told Simeon to go meet them. Simeon took the baby in his arms. He testified that this was the Savior. Then he blessed the baby and his parents and prophesied about Jesus' mission.

Anna was a prophetess who served in the temple. She was probably more than 100 years old. She also met Jesus and his parents. She thanked God for letting her see the Savior. When others wondered whether the Savior had come to Earth yet, Anna testified to them about Jesus (Luke 2:25–38).

Thought question: How would it feel to know the Savior had come, after waiting so long?

Scripture

And it had come to pass, yea, all things, every whit, according to the words of the prophets (3 Nephi 1:20).

Visual Aid:

GAPK 201
The Nativity

3. Jesus Christ restored His gospel through the Prophet Joseph Smith.

Scripture

Joseph Smith, the Prophet and Seer of the Lord, has done more, save Jesus only, for the salvation of men in this world, than any other man that ever lived in it (D&C 135:3).

When Jesus was on the earth, He organized His true Church. But He knew that it would not last on the earth. Long before, the prophet Amos had said that the Lord would send "a famine in the land, not a famine of bread, nor a thirst for water, but of hearing the words of the Lord" (Amos 8:11). A famine is a time when there is no food or water. People were starving to hear the true gospel of Jesus Christ. But no one had the authority or the truth.

In 1820, a young boy named Joseph Smith wanted to know the truth. He wanted to find God's true Church. When he prayed, Heavenly Father and Jesus Christ appeared to him. They told him that none of the churches was right. They commanded him to organize the true Church again (Joseph Smith—History 1:8-20).

At last the famine was over! Heavenly Father's true Church was on the earth again.

Thought question: How is wanting God's truth like feeling very hungry?

Visual Aid:

GAPK 403
The First Vision

4. Because I know that I am a child of God and that Jesus Christ is my Savior, I will . . .

When President Hinckley was a young boy, his father brought home a new Model T car. Cars were less advanced back then. The new car had no battery to power the lights. The power for the lights came from the engine. When the engine ran fast, the lights were bright. But if the engine slowed down, the lights grew dim.

President Hinckley said that the lights on the car are like our lives. "You have to stay on your feet and keep moving if you are going to have light in your life."[16]

We can follow President Hinckley's counsel by keeping the commandments with joy and energy. As we "keep moving" in the gospel, the Spirit can light our way through life.

Thought question: How can you "stay on your feet and keep moving" in life?

Scripture

But he that doeth truth cometh to the light, that his deeds may be made manifest, that they are wrought in God (John 3:21).

Visual Aid:

GAPK 520
Gordon B. Hinckley

References

1. John A. Widtsoe, ed., *Discourses of Brigham Young* (Salt Lake City: Bookcraft, 1954), 51.

2. Dieter F. Uchtdorf, "The Power of a Personal Testimony," *Ensign*, November 2006, 37–39.

3. *Gospel Principles* (Salt Lake City: The Church of Jesus Christ of Latter-Day Saints, 1997), 21.

4. Merrill J. Bateman, "A Pattern for All," *Ensign*, November 2005, 74.

5. Thomas S. Monson, "True to the Faith," *Ensign*, May 2006, 18–21.

6. Gordon B. Hinckley, "Forgiveness," *Ensign*, November 2005, 81.

7. Gordon B. Hinckley, "A Testimony Vibrant and True," *Ensign*, August 2005, 2.

8. Gordon B. Hinckley, "The Faith to Move Mountains," *Ensign*, November 2006, 82–85.

9. Boyd K. Packer, "The Holy Temple," *Ensign*, February 1995, 32.

10. Joseph Fielding Smith, ed., *Life of Joseph F. Smith, Sixth President of The Church of Jesus Christ of Latter-day Saints* (Salt Lake City: The Deseret News Press, 1938), 188–89.

11. Richard G. Scott, "Learning to Recognize Answers to Prayer," *Ensign*, November 1989, 30.

12. Dean L. Larsen, "Winding Up Our Spiritual Clocks," *Ensign*, November 1989, 61.

13. L. Tom Perry, "A Solemn Responsibility to Love and Care for Each Other," *Ensign*, June 2006, 88–92.

14. Luis Mella, "My Last Chance," *Ensign*, August 2007, 71–72.

15. Thomas S. Monson, "The Peril of Hidden Wedges," *Ensign*, July 2007, 2–7.

16. Gordon B. Hinckley, "Some Lessons I Learned as a Boy," *Ensign*, May 1993, 52.

About the Author

Lee Ann Setzer was born in the Mojave Desert in Southern California. She has lived in Utah for more than twenty years. She served in the Japan Sendai Mission and still likes raw fish. She graduated from Brigham Young University with a bachelor's and then a master's degree in speech-language pathology.

Lee Ann is the author of several books, including *I Am Ready for Baptism*, the Sariah McDuff series, *Tiny Talks* volumes 6 and 7, and *Gathered: A Novel of Ruth*.

Lee Ann and her husband have three children, who all like to talk and write. They live in Utah.